FRENCH COOKING

GALLERY BOOKS
An Imprint of W. H. Smith Publishers Inc.
112 Madison Avenue
New York City 10016

INTRODUCTION

The bureaucrats of France have divided the country, for offical purposes, into 95 départéments, rather like counties. The cooks of France have a better way. They still rely on the old names of the regions, each with its own contribution to the country's legendary cuisine.

Brittany is the home of crêpes, thin French pancakes. Normandy is famous for its rich cream and apples. Cider comes from those apples and Calvados, an incendiary brandy, comes from the cider. And the seas around the coasts provide an abundance of seafood.

Champagne's main contribution is obvious, but there are also rich dishes of Flemish influence coming from this region on the Belgian border.

Touraine and the Loire are known as the garden of France, with the finest fruits and vegetables and some of the loveliest wines.

Ile de France has Paris at its center, where hâute cuisine was born.

Alsace and Lorraine have been dominated by Germany more than once in their history and this is evident in many of their favorite dishes.

Burgundy and Bordeaux use their famous red and white wines to enhance their recipes, along with Dijon mustard from the former and truffles from the latter.

Franche Comté is a mountainous region that abounds with game and which produces robust dishes, many using its famous cheese.

Languedoc is on the Spanish border and its food shares many similarities with that of its neighbors, especially in the use of tomatoes, pepper and spicy sausage.

Provence is southern France, with all its color and warmth reflected in food such as Salade Niçoise and Ratatouille.

With the whole history of French cuisine before us and with only limited space, we didn't know where to begin, or end! Then we thought of the many well-loved classics, the ones that conjure up the essence of the French gastronomic experience. With those, we felt, we couldn't go wrong.

SERVES 6

QUICHE LORRAINE

The history of this egg and bacon flan goes back
to the 16th century in the Lorraine region. Traditionally
it doesn't contain cheese, but it's a tasty addition.

Pâte Brisée

½ cup butter
1½ cups all-purpose flour, sifted
Pinch salt
1 egg
2 tsps ice water

Filling

6 strips bacon, cut into large dice
1 tsp butter or margarine
2 shallots, finely chopped
2 eggs plus 2 egg yolks
1 cup heavy cream
Salt, pepper and grated nutmeg
¾ cup grated Gruyère cheese (optional)

Step 2 Use rolling pin to lift pastry into dish.

1. Preheat the oven to 375°F. To prepare the pastry, sift the flour and salt into a large bowl. Rub in the butter until the mixture looks like fine breadcrumbs - this may also be done in a food processor. Beat the egg lightly and mix into the flour by hand or with the machine. If the dough seems crumbly, add some of the water. Chill well before using.

2. Roll the pastry out to a circle about ¼ inch thick on a well-floured surface. Roll the pastry over a rolling pin and unroll it onto a 8-9 inch flan dish. Gently press the pastry into the bottom and up the sides of the dish, being careful not to stretch it. Trim off the excess pastry by running the rolling pin over the rim of the dish or using a sharp knife. Prick the bottom of the pastry lightly With a fork.

3. Place a circle of wax paper on top of the pastry and fill with dry beans, or rice. Bake for about 10 minutes, remove the paper and filling. Prick base again lightly and return to the oven for another 3 minutes or until just beginning to brown. Allow the pastry to cool while preparing the filling.

4. Place the bacon in a small frying pan and fry over gentle heat until the fat begins to run. Raise the heat and cook until lightly browned and crisp. Place the bacon on paper towels to drain and add the butter to the pan if insufficient fat left. Add the chopped shallots and cook until just beginning to color. Remove to the paper towel to drain with the bacon.

5. Beat the eggs and extra yolks, cream and seasonings together in a large bowl. Scatter the bacon and shallots over the bottom of the pastry case and ladle the custard filling on top of it. If using cheese, add with the custard.

6. Bake in the top half of the oven for about 25 minutes, or until the custard has puffed and browned and a knife inserted into the center comes out clean. Allow to cool slightly and then remove from the dish, or serve directly from the dish.

Cook's Notes

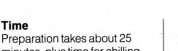

Time
Preparation takes about 25 minutes, plus time for chilling the pastry. Cooking takes about 40 minutes.

Preparation
Baking a pastry case without a filling is called baking blind.
By pricking the bottom of the pastry, lining it with paper and filling with rice or beans you help the pastry hold its shape.

Variation
Use basic pastry and custard recipes, but substitute other ingredients such as ham, shellfish or vegetables for the bacon.

MAKES 1 OMELET

OMELETTE ROUSSILLON

Roussillon is on France's border with Spain.
The Spanish influence is evident in the use of
tomatoes and peppers combined with eggs.

3 eggs
Salt and pepper
1 tbsp butter or margarine
¼ green pepper, cut into small dice
2 tomatoes, peeled, seeded and roughly chopped
2oz ham, cut into small dice

1. Break the eggs into a bowl, season with salt and pepper and beat to mix thoroughly. Heat an omelet pan and drop in the butter, swirling it so that it coats the bottom and sides. When the butter stops foaming, add pepper and ham. Cook for 1-2 minutes to soften slightly, and add the tomatoes.

2. Pour in the eggs and, as they begin to cook, push the cooked portion with the flat of the fork to allow the uncooked portion underneath. Continue to lift the eggs and shake the pan to prevent them from sticking.

3. When the egg on top is still slightly creamy, fold ⅓ of the omelet to the center and tip it out of the pan onto a warm serving dish, folded side down. Serve immediately.

Step 2 Push eggs with fork to let uncooked portion fall to the bottom of the pan.

Step 3 Fold ⅓ of the omelet to the middle.

Cook's Notes

Time
15 minutes preparation, 4-5 minutes cooking.

Preparation
To peel tomatoes, drop into boiling water for the count of 5 and remove to cold water. This loosens the peel.

Variations
Prepare the omelet in the same way, but use other ingredients such as mushrooms, chopped fresh herbs or spinach. If filling with cheese, sprinkle on before folding the omelet.

Serving Ideas
Accompany with French bread and a salad for a light lunch. May also be served as a first course.

SERVES 4-6

POTAGE À L'OIGNON GRATINÉ

Originally a Parisian specialty, every region in
France now has a recipe for onion soup.

¼ cup butter or margarine
2lbs onions, peeled and thinly sliced
2 tsps sugar
Pinch salt and pepper
1½ tbsps flour
1 tsp dried thyme
7 cups brown stock
½ cup dry white wine

Croûtes

12 1 inch slices French bread
1 tbsp olive oil
2 cups grated Gruyère cheese

Step 1 Brown the onions in a large saucepan with butter and sugar.

1. Melt the butter in a large saucepan over a moderate heat. Stir in the onions and add the sugar. Cook, un-covered, over low heat, stirring occasionally, for 20-30 minutes or until the onions are golden brown.

2. Sprinkle the flour over the onions and cook for 2-3 minutes. Pour on the stock and stir to blend the flour. Add salt, pepper and thyme and return the soup to low heat. Simmer, partially covered, for another 30-40 minutes. Allow the soup to stand while preparing the croûtes.

Step 3 Brush both sides of bread with olive oil and bake until lightly browned.

3. Brush each side of the slices of bread lightly with olive oil and place them on a baking sheet. Bake in a preheated oven, 325°F, for about 15 minutes. Turn the slices over and bake for a further 15 minutes, or until the bread is dry and lightly browned.

Step 4 Place the croûtes on soup and sprinkle with cheese.

4. To serve, skim fat from the soup and ladle soup into a tureen or individual soup bowls. Place the croûtes on top of the soup and sprinkle over the grated cheese. Place the soup in a hot oven and bake for 10-20 minutes, or until the cheese has melted. Brown under a preheated broiler, if desired, before serving.

Cook's Notes

Time
Preparation takes about 20 minutes. Cooking takes about 50-60 minutes - 40 minutes for the soup, 30 minutes for the croûtes and 10-20 minutes to melt the cheese.

Cook's Tip
The addition of sugar helps the onions to brown.

SERVES 10

PÂTÉ DE CAMPAGNE

This is the pâté of French restaurants
known also as pâté maison or terrine
de chef. It should be coarse textured.

¾lb pork liver, skinned and ducts removed
¾lb pork, coarsely ground
4oz veal, coarsely ground
8oz pork fat, coarsely ground
1 clove garlic, crushed
2 shallots, finely chopped
8oz bacon strips, rind and bones removed
3 tbsps cognac
½ tsp ground allspice
Salt and freshly ground black pepper
1 tsp chopped fresh thyme or sage
4oz smoked tongue or ham, cut into ¼ inch cubes
2 tbsps heavy cream
1 large bay leaf

Step 3 Stretch the strips of bacon to line the terrine.

Step 5 Weight down the pâté with cans or scale weights.

1. Preheat the oven to 350°F.

2. Place the liver in a food processor and process once or twice to chop roughly. Add the ground meats and fat, shallots, garlic, cognac, allspice, salt and pepper and thyme and process once or twice to mix. Do not over-work the mixture; it should be coarse.

3. Stretch the strips of bacon with the back of a knife and line a terrine, metal baking pan or ovenproof glass dish. Stir the cream and the cubed tongue or ham into the meat mixture by hand and press it into the dish on top of the bacon.
Place the bay leaf on top and fold over any overlapping edges of bacon.

4. Cover the dish with a tight-fitting lid or two layers of foil

and place the dish in a bain marie (dish of hand hot water) to come halfway up the sides of the terrine. Bake the pâté for 2 hours, or until the juices are clear. When it is done, remove it from the oven and remove the foil or lid.

5. Cover with fresh foil and weight down the pâté with cans of food or balance scale weights. Allow to cool at room temperature and then refrigerate the pâté, still weighted, until completely chilled and firm.

6. To serve, remove the weights and foil. Turn the pâté out and scrape off the fat. Slice through the bacon into thin slices.

Cook's Notes

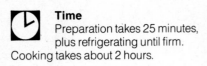

Time
Preparation takes 25 minutes, plus refrigerating until firm. Cooking takes about 2 hours.

Serving Ideas
The French often serve pâté with small pickled onions, and cornichons (small pickled gherkins). Serve as a first course with French bread or buttered toast, or with bread and salad for a light lunch.

Freezing
Cool and freeze in the dish. Pack well, label and store for up to 3 months. Allow to defrost in the refrigerator.

SERVES 4-6

Gougère au Jambon

This savory pastry dish originated in Burgundy, but is also popular in the Champagne district and indeed in many other districts as well. Serve it as an appetizer or main course.

Choux Pastry

½ cup water
4 tbsps butter or margarine
½ cup all-purpose flour, sifted
2 eggs, beaten
½ cup cheese, finely diced
Pinch salt, pepper and dry mustard

Ham Salpicon —chicken

1 tbsp butter or margarine
1 tbsp flour
½ cup stock
2oz mushrooms, sliced
2 tsps chopped fresh herbs
Salt and pepper
4oz cooked ham, cut into julienne strips
2 tbsps grated cheese and dry breadcrumbs mixed

Step 4 Beat in the egg gradually, but thoroughly.

Step 5 Spoon up the sides of the dish and fill the center with the salpicon.

1. Preheat oven to 400°F. Place the water for the pastry in a small saucepan. Cut the butter into small pieces and add to the water. Bring slowly to boil, making sure that the butter is completely melted before the water comes to a rapid boil. Turn up the heat and allow to boil rapidly for 30 seconds.

2. Sift the flour with a pinch of salt onto a sheet of paper. Take the pan off the heat and tip all the flour in at once. Stir quickly and vigorously until the mixture comes away from the sides of the pan. Spread onto a plate to cool.

3. Melt the butter in a small saucepan for the salpicon and add the flour. Cook for 1-2 minutes until pale straw colored. Gradually whisk in the stock until smooth. Add a pinch of salt and pepper and the chopped herbs. Stir in the sliced mushrooms and ham and set aside.

4. To continue with the pastry, add salt, pepper and dry mustard to the paste and return it to the saucepan. Gradually add the egg to the paste mixture, beating well between each addition–this may be done by hand, with an electric mixer or in a food processor. It may not be necessary to add all the egg. The mixture should be smooth and shiny and hold its shape when ready. If it is still too thick, beat in the remaining egg. Stir in the diced cheese by hand.

5. Spoon the mixture into a large ovenproof dish or 4 individual dishes, pushing the mixture slightly up the sides of the dish and leaving a well in the center. Fill the center with the ham salpicon and scatter over 2 tbsps grated cheese and dry breadcrumbs, mixed. Bake until the pastry is puffed and browned. Serve immediately.

Cook's Notes

Serving Ideas
Cooked in individual dishes, this makes a nice first course for 6. Cooked in a large dish this makes a main course for 4 with a salad or vegetables.

Time
Preparation takes about 30 minutes, cooking takes approximately 30-45 minutes if cooked in one large dish, 15-20 minutes for small individual dishes.

Variations
Vegetables, chicken, game or shellfish can be substituted for the ham.

SERVES 4

ARTICHAUTS AIOLI

Home-made mayonnaise is in a class by itself.
With the addition of garlic, it makes a perfect sauce
for artichokes – a typically Provençal appetizer.

4 medium-sized globe artichokes
1 slice lemon
1 bay leaf
Pinch salt

Sauce Aioli

2 egg yolks
1 cup olive oil
2 cloves garlic, peeled and crushed
Salt, pepper and lemon juice to taste
Chervil leaves to garnish

Step 1 Trim the pointed ends from all the leaves of the artichoke.

Step 2 Add the oil to the egg yolks in a thin, steady stream to prevent curdling.

Step 3 Pull away one of the bottom leaves to see if the artichoke is cooked.

1. To prepare the artichokes, break off the stems and twist to remove any tough fibers. Trim the base so that the artichokes will stand upright. Trim the points from all the leaves and wash the artichokes well. Bring a large saucepan or stock pot full of water to the boil with the slice of lemon and bay leaf. Add a pinch of salt and, when the water is boiling, add the artichokes. Allow to cook for 25 minutes over a moderate heat. While the artichokes are cooking, prepare the sauce.

2. Whisk the egg yolks and garlic with a pinch of salt and pepper in a deep bowl or in a liquidizer or food processor. Add the olive oil a few drops at a time while whisking by hand, or in a thin steady stream with the machine running. If preparing the sauce by hand, once half the oil is added, the remainder may be added in a thin, steady stream. Add lemon juice once the sauce becomes very thick. When all the oil has been added, adjust the seasoning and add more lemon juice to taste.

3. When the artichokes are cooked, the bottom leaves will pull away easily. Remove them from the water with a draining spoon and drain upside-down on paper towels or in a colander. Allow to cool and serve with the sauce aioli. Garnish with chervil.

Cook's Notes

Time
Preparation will take approximately 30 minutes and cooking approximately 25 minutes.

Cook's Tip
If this sauce or other mayonnaise needs to be thinned for coating, mix with a little hot water. A damp cloth under the mixing bowl will stop it spinning when making mayonnaise by hand.

Watchpoint
Sauce will curdle if oil is added too quickly. If it does, whisk another egg yolk and gradually beat curdled mixture into it. Sauce should come together again.

Serving Ideas
To eat, peel the leaves off one at a time and dip the fleshy part of the leaf into the sauce. Work down to the thistle or choke and remove with a teaspoon. Break artichoke bottom into pieces and dip into sauce.

SERVES 6-8

RATATOUILLE

This is probably one of the most familiar dishes from southern France. Either hot or cold, it's full of the warm sun of Provence.

2 eggplants, sliced and scored on both sides
4-6 zucchini, depending on size
3-6 tbsps olive oil
2 onions, peeled and thinly sliced
2 green peppers, seeded and cut into 1 inch pieces
2 tsps chopped fresh basil or 1 tsp dried basil
1 large clove garlic, crushed
2lbs ripe tomatoes, peeled and quartered
Salt and pepper
½ cup dry white wine

1. Lightly salt the eggplant slices and place on paper towels to drain for about 30 minutes. Rinse and pat dry. Slice the zucchini thickly and set them aside.

2. Pour 3 tbsps of the olive oil into a large frying pan and when hot, lightly brown the onions, green peppers and zucchini slices. Remove the vegetables to a casserole and add the eggplant slices to the frying pan or saucepan. Cook to brown both sides lightly and place in the casserole with the other vegetables. Add extra oil while frying the vegetables as needed.

3. Add the garlic and tomatoes to the oil and cook for 1 minute. Add the garlic and tomatoes to the rest of the vegetables along with any remaining olive oil in the frying pan. Add basil, salt, pepper and wine and bring to the boil over moderate heat. Cover and reduce to simmering. If the vegetables need moisture during cooking, add a little white wine.

Step 1 Score and salt the eggplants and leave to drain.

Step 2 Brown all the vegetables lightly.

Step 3 Combine all the ingredients and simmer gently.

4. When the vegetables are tender, remove them from the casserole to a serving dish and boil any remaining liquid in the pan rapidly to reduce to about 2 tbsps. Pour over the ratatouille to serve.

Cook's Notes

Time
Leave eggplants to stand 30 minutes while preparing remaining vegetables. Cook combined ingredients for approximately 35 minutes.

Cook's Tip
Vegetables in this stew are traditionally served quite soft. If crisper vegetables are desired, shorten the cooking time but make sure the eggplant is thoroughly cooked.

SERVES 6

FÈVES AU JAMBON

Touraine, where this dish comes from, is often called the "Garden of France." Some of the finest vegetables in the country are grown there.

2lbs lima beans
½ cup heavy cream
2oz ham, cut into thin strips
1 tbsps chopped parsley or chervil

1. If using fresh beans, remove them from their pods. Cook the beans in boiling salted water until tender, drain and keep warm.

2. Combine the cream and ham in a small saucepan. Add a pinch of salt and pepper and bring to the boil. Boil rapidly for 5 minutes to thicken the cream.

Step 2 Reduce the cream to thicken by boiling.

Step 3 Peel off outer skins of beans before adding to cream and ham.

Step 1 Remove fresh lima beans from their pods.

3. If desired, peel the outer skins from the beans before tossing with the cream and ham. Add parsley or chervil, adjust the seasoning and reheat if necessary. Serve immediately.

Cook's Notes

Time
Preparation takes 20-30 minutes, beans take approximately 15 minutes to cook.

Variation
Fresh peas may be used instead of beans, and cooked for 20-25 minutes.

Cook's Tip
The finished dish has better color if the beans are peeled.

SERVES 4

TOMATES À LA LANGUEDOCIENNE

This dish from the Languedoc region of southern France is similar to Provençal tomatoes, but is not as strong in flavor.

Step 2 Chop stuffing finely.

4 large ripe tomatoes
2 slices white bread, crusts removed
1 clove garlic, crushed
2 tbsps olive oil
1 tbsp chopped parsley
2 tsp chopped thyme or marjoram
Salt and pepper

1. Cut the tomatoes in half and score the cut surface. Sprinkle with salt and leave upside-down in a colander to drain. Allow the tomatoes to drain for 1-2 hours. Rinse the tomatoes and scoop out most of the juice and pulp.

2. Mix the olive oil and garlic together and brush both sides of the bread with the mixture, leaving it to soften. Chop the herbs and the bread together until well mixed.

Step 3 Press in as much stuffing as possible.

Step 1 Scoop out seeds and juice to create space for the stuffing.

3. Press the filling into the tomatoes and sprinkle with any remaining garlic and olive oil mixture.

4. Cook the tomatoes in an ovenproof dish under a preheated broiler under low heat for the first 5 minutes. Then raise the dish or the heat to brown the tomatoes on top. Serve immediately.

Cook's Notes

Time
Preparation takes about 15 minutes, tomatoes need 1-2 hours to drain. Cooking takes approximately 5-8 minutes.

Preparation
Can be prepared up to broiling and finished off just before serving.

Serving Ideas
Serve as a first course or a side dish. Especially nice with lamb or beef.

SERVES 4-6

HARICOTS VERTS À L'OIGNON

These slender green beans are the classic French vegetable. Quickly blanched, then refreshed under cold water, they can be reheated and still stay beautifully green.

1lb green beans
1oz butter
1 medium onion
Salt and pepper

Step 2 Finely chop the onion.

Step 1 Top and tail the beans, but leave them whole.

Step 3 Fry the onion in moderate heat until lightly browned.

1. Top and tail the beans.

2. Cook the beans whole in boiling salted water for about 8-10 minutes. Meanwhile, finely chop the onion.

3. Melt the butter and fry the finely chopped onion until lightly brown. Drain the beans and toss them over heat to dry. Pour the butter and onions over the beans and season with salt and pepper. Serve immediately.

Cook's Notes

Watchpoint
Do not brown the onions too much as this will make them taste bitter.

Time
Preparation takes about 15 minutes, cooking takes 8-10 minutes.

Preparation
Trim the beans with a sharp knife or kitchen scissors in large handfuls.

SERVES 6

POMMES DAUPHINÉ

The food from the mountainous province of Dauphiné is robust fare. Comté is the finest cheese of the area and like Gruyère it is creamy rather than stringy when melted.

1 clove garlic, peeled and crushed with the flat of a knife
2 tbsps butter
2¼lbs potatoes, peeled and thinly sliced
½ cup light cream
Salt and pepper
1½ cups grated Comté or Gruyère cheese
⅓ cup butter cut into very small dice

1. Preheat the oven to 400°F. Rub the bottom and sides of a heavy baking dish with the crushed clove of garlic. Grease the bottom and sides liberally with the butter. Use a dish that can also be employed as a serving dish.

2. Spread half of the potato slices in the bottom of the dish, sprinkle with cheese, salt and pepper and dot with the butter dice. Top with the remaining slices of potato, neatly

Step 2 Layer the potatoes with cheese and seasonings.

Step 3 Pour cream into the side of the dish.

Step 1 Rub the dish with garlic and butter well.

arranged. Sprinkle with the remaining cheese, salt, pepper and butter.

3. Pour the cream into the side of the dish around the potatoes.

4. Cook in the top part of the oven for 30-40 minutes, or until the potatoes are tender and the top is nicely browned. Serve immediately.

Cook's Notes

Serving Ideas
A delicious side dish with poultry or roast meats, especially gammon.

Cook's Tip
Rubbing the dish with garlic gives just a hint of flavor.

Time
Preparation takes 25 minutes, cooking takes 30-40 minutes.

SERVES 4

POULET GRILLÉ AU LIMON

Crisp chicken with a tang of limes makes an elegant
yet quickly-made entrée. From the warm regions of
southern France, it is perfect for a summer meal.

2 2lb chickens
4 limes
1 tsp basil
⅓ cup olive oil
Salt, pepper and sugar

1. Remove the leg ends, neck and wing tips from the
chicken and discard them.

2. Split the chicken in half, cutting away the backbone
completely and discarding it.

3. Loosen the ball and socket joint in the leg and flatten
each half of the chicken by hitting it with the flat side of a
cleaver.

4. Season the chicken on both sides with salt and pepper
and sprinkle over the basil. Place the chicken in a shallow
dish and pour over 2 tbsps of olive oil. Squeeze the juice
from 2 of the limes over the chicken. Cover and leave to
marinate in the refrigerator for 4 hours.

5. Heat the broiler to its highest setting and preheat the
oven to 375°F. Remove the chicken from the marinade and
place in the broiler pan. Cook one side until golden brown
and turn the pieces over. Sprinkle with 1 tbsp olive oil and
brown the other side.

6. Place the chicken in a roasting dish, sprinkle with the

Step 2 Split the
chicken in half
and cut out the
backbone.

Step 3 Bend
chicken leg back
to loosen ball and
socket joint.

remaining oil and roast in the oven for about 25 minutes.
Peel the remaining limes and slice them thinly. When the
chicken is cooked, place the lime slices on top and sprinkle
lightly with sugar. Place under the broiler for a few minutes
to caramelize the sugar and cook the limes. Place in a
serving dish and spoon over any remaining marinade and
the cooking juices. Serve immediately.

Cook's Notes

Time
Preparation takes about 25
minutes, plus 4 hours
marinating, cooking takes about 35
minutes.

Watchpoint
Sugar will burn and turn bitter
quickly, so watch carefully
while broiling.

Variation
If limes are too expensive, use
lemons instead. Vary the
choice of herb.

Serving Ideas
Tomato salad makes a good
accompaniment.

Preparation
Chicken can be prepared and
marinated overnight in the
refrigerator.

Cook's Tip
Marinating the chicken adds
moisture as well as flavor.

SERVES 4

Poulet Sauté Vallée d'Auge

This dish contains all the ingredients that Normandy is famous for - butter, cream, apples and Calvados.

¼ cup butter or margarine
2 tbsps oil
3lbs chicken, cut into eight pieces
4 tbsps Calvados
⅓ cup chicken stock
2 apples, peeled, cored and coarsely chopped
2 sticks celery, finely chopped
1 shallot, finely chopped
½ tsp dried thyme, crumbled
⅓ cup heavy cream
2 egg yolks, lightly beaten
Salt and white pepper

Garnish

1 bunch watercress or small parsley sprigs
2 apples, quartered, cored and cut into cubes
2 tbsps butter
Sugar

Step 1 Brown the chicken a few pieces at a time, skin side down first.

Step 4 Cook diced apple until it begins to caramelize.

1. Melt half the butter and all of the oil in a large sauté pan over moderate heat. When the foam begins to subside, brown the chicken, a few pieces at a time, skin side down first. When all the chicken is browned, pour off most of the fat from the pan and return the chicken to the pan.

2. Pour the Calvados into a ladle or small saucepan and warm over gentle heat. Ignite with a match and pour, while still flaming, over the chicken. Shake the sauté pan gently until the flames subside. If the Calvados should flare up, cover the pan immediately with the lid.

3. Pour over the stock and scrape any browned chicken juices from the bottom of the pan. Set the chicken aside. Melt the remaining butter in a small saucepan or frying pan. Cook the chopped apples, shallot and celery and the thyme for about 10 minutes or until soft but not brown.

Spoon over the chicken and return the pan to the high heat. Bring to the boil, then reduce heat, cover the pan and simmer 50 minutes. When the chicken is cooked, beat the eggs and cream. With a whisk, gradually beat in some of the hot sauce. Pour the mixture back into a saucepan and cook over a low heat for 2-3 minutes, stirring constantly until the sauce thickens and coats the back of a spoon. Season the sauce with salt and white pepper and set aside while preparing the garnish.

4. Put the remaining butter in a small frying pan and when foaming, add the apple. Toss over a high heat until beginning to soften. Sprinkle with sugar and cook until the apple begins to caramelize. To serve, coat the chicken with the sauce and decorate with watercress or parsley. Spoon the caramelized apples over the chicken.

Cook's Notes

 Time
Preparation takes 25-30 minutes, cooking takes 55-60 minutes.

 Watchpoint
Do not allow the sauce to boil once the egg and cream is added or it will curdle.

 Serving Ideas
Serve with sauté potatoes and fresh young peas.

SERVES 4

Coq au Vin

Originating from the Burgundy region, this dish is
probably the most famous chicken recipe in all of France.
It is very rich, definitely a cold weather meal.

8oz thick cut bacon strips
1½ cups water
2 tbsps butter or margarine
12-16 button onions or shallots
8oz mushrooms, left whole if small, quartered if large
1½ cups dry red wine
3lb chicken, cut into eight pieces
3 tbsps brandy
1 bouquet garni
1 clove garlic, crushed
3 tbsps flour
1½ cups chicken stock
2 tbsps chopped parsley
4 slices bread, crusts removed
Oil for frying
Salt and pepper

1. Preheat oven to 350°F. Cut the bacon into strips about ¼ inch thick. Bring water the boil and blanch the bacon by simmering for 5 minutes. Remove the bacon with a draining spoon and dry on paper towels. Re-boil the water and drop in the onions. Allow them to boil rapidly for 2-3 minutes and then plunge into cold water and peel. Set the onions aside with the bacon.

2. Melt half the butter in a large frying pan over moderate heat and add the bacon and onions. Fry over high heat, stirring frequently and shaking the pan, until the bacon and onions are golden brown. Remove them with a draining spoon and leave on paper towels. Add the remaining butter to the saucepan and cook the mushrooms for 1-2 minutes. Remove them and set them aside with the onions and bacon.

3. Reheat the frying pan and brown the chicken, a few pieces at a time. When all the chicken is browned, transfer it to a large ovenproof casserole.

Step 1 Cut the bacon into small strips and blanch to remove excess salt.

4. Pour the wine into a small saucepan and boil it to reduce to about 1 cup. Pour the brandy into a small saucepan or ladle and warm over low heat. Ignite with a match and pour the brandy (while still flaming) over the chicken. Shake the casserole carefully until the flames die down. If the brandy should flare up, cover quickly with the casserole lid. Add the bouquet garni and garlic to the casserole.

5. Pour off all but 1 tbsp of fat from the frying pan and stir in the flour. Cook over gentle heat, scraping any of the browned chicken juices from the bottom of the pan. Pour in the reduced wine and add the stock. Bring the sauce to the boil over high heat, stirring constantly until thickened. Strain over the chicken in the casserole and cover tightly.

6. Place in the oven and cook for 20 minutes. After that time, add the bacon, onions and mushrooms and continue cooking for a further 15-20 minutes, or until the chicken is tender. Remove the bouquet garni and season with salt and pepper.

7. Cut each of the bread slices into 4 triangles. Heat enough oil in a large frying pan to cover the triangles of bread. When the oil is very hot, add the bread triangles two at a time and fry until golden brown and crisp. Drain on paper towels. To serve, arrange the chicken in a deep dish, pour over the sauce and vegetables and arrange the fried bread croûtes around the outside of the dish. Sprinkle with chopped parsley.

Cook's Notes

 Watchpoint
Make sure the oil for frying the croûtes is hot enough when the bread is added, otherwise croûtes can be very oily.

Cook's Tip
Blanching the bacon in boiling water removes excess saltiness. Boiling the onions makes them easier to peel.

Time
Preparation takes 30-40 minutes, cooking takes about 50 minutes.

SERVES 4

POULET FRICASSÉE

This is a white stew, enriched and thickened with an egg and cream mixture which is called a liaison in French cooking.

3lb chicken, quartered and skinned
¼ cup butter or margarine
2 tbsps flour
2 cups chicken stock
1 bouquet garni
12-16 small onions, peeled
12oz button mushrooms, whole if small, quartered if large
Juice and grated rind of ½ lemon
2 egg yolks
⅓ cup heavy cream
2 tbsps chopped parsley and thyme
Salt and pepper
3 tbsps milk (optional)
Garnish with lemon slices

Step 3 Tie a bay leaf, sprig of thyme and parsley stalks together to make a bouquet garni.

1. Melt 3 tbsps of the butter in a large sauté pan or frying pan. Place in the chicken in 1 layer and cook over gentle heat for about 5 minutes, or until the chicken is no longer pink. Do not allow the chicken to brown. If necessary, cook the chicken in two batches. When the chicken is sufficiently cooked, remove it from the pan and set aside.

2. Stir the flour into the butter remaining in the pan and cook over very low heat, stirring continuously for about 1 minute, or until a pale straw color. Remove the pan from the heat and gradually beat in the chicken stock. When blended smoothly, add lemon juice and rind, return the pan to the heat and bring to the boil, whisking constantly. Reduce the heat and allow the sauce to simmer for 1 minute.

3. Return the chicken to the pan with any juices that have accumulated and add the bouquet garni. The sauce should almost cover the chicken. If it does not, add more stock or water. Bring to the boil, cover the pan and reduce the heat. Allow the chicken to simmer gently for 30 minutes.

4. Meanwhile, melt the remaining butter in a small frying pan, add the onions, cover and cook very gently for 10 minutes. Do not allow the onions to brown. Remove the onions from the pan with a draining spoon and add to the chicken. Cook the mushrooms in the remaining butter for 2 minutes. Set the mushrooms aside and add them to the chicken 10 minutes before the end of cooking.

5. Test the chicken by piercing a thigh portion with a sharp knife. If the juices run clear, the chicken is cooked. Transfer chicken and vegetables to a serving plate and discard the bouquet garni. Skim the sauce of any fat and boil it rapidly to reduce by almost half.

6. Blend the egg yolks and cream together and whisk in several spoonfuls of the hot sauce. Return the egg yolk and cream mixture to the remaining sauce and cook gently for 2-3 minutes. Stir the sauce constantly and do not allow it to boil. If very thick, add milk. Adjust the seasoning, stir in the parsley and spoon over the chicken in a serving dish. Garnish with lemon slices.

Cook's Notes

Time
Preparation takes about 30 minutes, cooking takes about 30-40 minutes.

Serving Idea
Serve with boiled potatoes or rice.

Cook's Tip
Pour boiling water over the onions and leave to soak 10 minutes to make them easier to peel. Alternatively, prepare as for Coq au Vin.

Watchpoint
A fricassée is a white stew. Cook gently to avoid browning the ingredients.

SERVES 4-6

SALADE NIÇOISE

Almost everyone knows what Salade Niçoise is, but there are so many variations that it need never be ordinary.

1 head Romaine lettuce
2 hard-boiled eggs, quartered
2 large tomatoes, quartered
6 anchovy fillets
10 pitted black olives
1 tbsp capers
¼ cucumber, diced but not peeled
1 can tuna fish, drained
4 large artichoke hearts, quartered

Dressing

⅓ cup olive oil
2 tbsps white or red wine vinegar
½ clove garlic, crushed
1 tsp mustard
Salt, pepper and lemon juice

Step 2 If anchovy fillets are thick, cut in half. Eggs, tomatoes, and artichoke hearts may be cut into smaller pieces if desired.

Step 2 Whisk the dressing ingredients well to blend thoroughly.

1. Wash the lettuce well, pat dry and break into bite-size pieces.

2. Prepare the remaining ingredients and toss with the lettuce in a large bowl, taking care not to break up the eggs. Mix the dressing ingredients together and whisk until well emulsified. Pour the dressing over the salad just before serving.

Step 1 Break well washed lettuce into bite-sized pieces.

Cook's Notes

 Serving Ideas
Makes a light lunch with French bread or a first course.

 Time
Preparation takes about 20 minutes, cooking approximately 9-10 minutes to hard-boil the eggs.

 Variations
Add cubed new potatoes or lightly cooked green beans or lima beans. Substitute shrimp for tuna, if desired.

 Preparation
If cooking eggs in advance, leave them in cold water to prevent a gray ring forming around the yolks.

SERVES 4

MOULES MARINIÈRE

Brittany and Normandy are famous for mussels and for cream
and so cooks combined the two in one perfect seafood dish.

3lbs mussels
1½ cups dry cider or white wine
4 shallots, finely chopped
1 clove garlic, crushed
1 bouquet garni
½ cup heavy cream
3 tbsps butter, cut into small pieces
2 tbsps finely chopped parsley

1. Scrub the mussels well and remove the beards and any barnacles from the shells. Discard any mussels that have cracked shells and do not open when lightly tapped. Put the mussels into a large bowl and soak in cold water for at least 1 hour. Meanwhile, chop the parsley very finely.

2. Bring the cider or wine to the boil in a large stock pot and add the shallots, garlic and bouquet garni. Add the mussels, cover the pan and cook for 5 minutes. Shake the pan or stir the mussels around frequently until the shells open. Lift out the mussels into a large soup tureen or individual serving bowls. Discard any mussels that have not opened.

3. Reduce the cooking liquid by about half and strain into another saucepan. Add the cream and bring to the boil to thicken slightly. Beat in the butter, a few pieces at a time. Adjust the seasoning, add the parsley and pour the sauce over the mussels to serve.

Step 1 Break off thick stems from parsley and chop leaves very finely.

Step 2 Whilst cooking the mussels, stir or shake them frequently until the shells open.

Step 3 Beat the butter into the thickened cream and cooking liquid, a few pieces at a time.

Cook's Notes

Preparation
Soak mussels with a handful of flour or cornmeal in the water. They will then expel sand and take up the flour or cornmeal, which plumps them up.

Serving Ideas
Serve as a first course with French bread, or double the quantity of mussels to serve for a light main course.

Time
Preparation takes about 30 minutes, cooking takes about 15 minutes.

SERVES 4

Raie au Beurre Noir

It is amazing how the addition of simple ingredients
like browned butter, vinegar, capers and parsley can
turn an ordinary fish into a French masterpiece.

4 wings of skate
1 slice onion
2 parsley stalks
Pinch salt
6 black peppercorns

Beurre Noir

4 tbsps butter
2 tbsps white wine vinegar
1 tbsp capers
1 tbsp chopped parsley (optional)

Step 1 Place the skate in a pan with the poaching liquid and flavouring ingredients.

1. Place the skate in one layer in a large, deep pan. Completely cover with water and add the onion, parsley stalks, salt and peppercorns. Bring gently to the boil with pan uncovered. Allow to simmer 15-20 minutes, or until the skate is done.

2. Lift the fish out onto a serving dish and remove the skin and any large pieces of bone. Take care not to break up the fish.

Step 2 Carefully remove any skin or large bones from the cooked fish, with a small knife.

3. Place the butter in a small pan and cook over high heat until it begins to brown. Add the capers and immediately remove the butter from the heat. Add the vinegar, which will cause the butter to bubble. Add parsley, if using, and pour immediately over the fish to serve.

Step 3 Pour sizzling butter over the fish to serve.

Cook's Notes

Variations
Chopped black olives, shallots or mushrooms may be used instead of or in addition to the capers. Add lemon juice instead of vinegar, if desired.

Cook's Tip
When the skate is done, it will pull away from the bones in long strips.

Time
Preparation takes about 20 minutes, cooking takes 15-20 minutes for the fish and about 5 minutes to brown the butter.

SERVES 4

ROUGETS À LA PROVENÇALE

Red Mullet is a very attractive fish, with a flavor quite
like shrimp. It is also known as "woodcock of the sea"
because it is often served with the liver left inside.

2 tbsps olive oil
1 clove garlic, crushed
2 shallots, finely chopped
1lb ripe tomatoes, peeled, seeded and sliced
2 tsps chopped marjoram and parsley mixed
⅓ cup dry white wine
Salt, pepper and pinch saffron
Oil for frying
2 small bulbs fennel, quartered and cored
4 red mullet, about 6oz each
Flour mixed with salt and pepper

Step 3 To scale fish, run the blunt end of a knife from the tail to the head.

Step 3 Remove the fins with kitchen scissors.

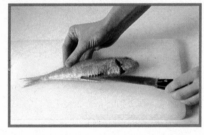

Step 3 Gut the fish, cut along the stomach and remove insides, leaving liver if desired.

1. Heat 2 tbsps olive oil in a deep saucepan and add the garlic and shallots. Cook 1-2 minutes to soften slightly, then add tomatoes, herbs, wine, salt, pepper and saffron. Allow to simmer, uncovered, for 30 minutes and set aside while preparing the fennel and fish.

2. Pour about 4 tbsps oil into a large frying pan or sauté pan. Place over moderate heat and add the fennel. Cook quickly until the fennel is slightly browned. Lower the heat and cook a further 5-10 minutes to soften the fennel.

3. Scale the fish, remove the gills and clean, leaving in the liver if desired. Wash the fish and dry thoroughly. Trim the fins and roll the fish in seasoned flour, shaking off the excess.

4. When the fennel is tender, remove it from the pan and set it aside. Fry the fish until golden brown on both sides, about 2-3 minutes per side. Arrange the fish in a warm serving dish and surround with the fennel. Reheat the sauce and spoon over the fish. Serve remaining sauce separately.

Cook's Notes

Time
Preparation takes about 30 minutes unless the fish are already cleaned. Cooking takes approximately 40 minutes.

Watchpoint
Red mullet spoils quickly, so use on day of purchase.

Cook's Tip
Saffron is expensive, so use a pinch of turmeric as a substitute for color.

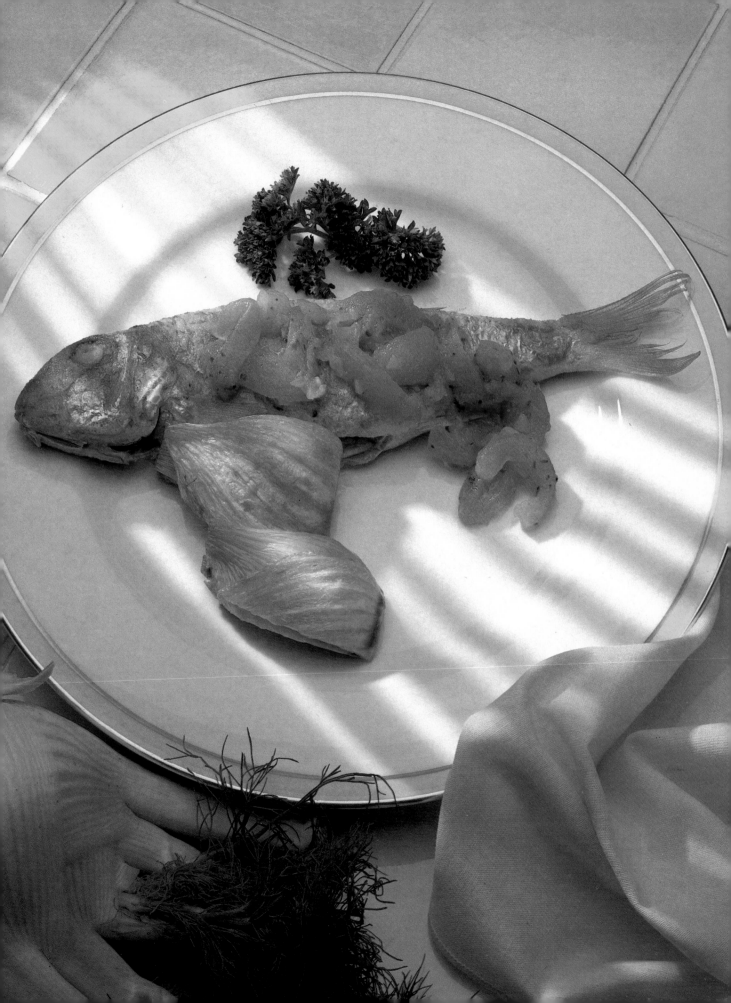

SERVES 4

TRUITE MEUNIÈRE AUX HERBES

The miller (meunier) caught trout fresh from the mill stream and his wife used the flour which was on hand to dredge them with, or so the story goes.

4 even-sized trout, cleaned and trimmed
Flour
Salt and pepper
½ cup butter
Juice of 1 lemon
2 tbsps chopped fresh herbs such as parsley, chervil, tarragon, thyme or marjoram
Lemon wedges to garnish

1. Trim the trout tails to make them more pointed. Rinse the trout well.

2. Dredge the trout with flour and shake off the excess. Season with salt and pepper. Heat half the butter in a very large sauté pan and, when foaming, place in the trout. It may be necessary to cook the trout in two batches to avoid overcrowding the pan.

3. Cook over fairly high heat on both sides to brown evenly. Depending on size, the trout should take 5-8 minutes per side to cook. The dorsal fin will pull out easily when the trout are cooked. Remove the trout to a serving dish and keep them warm.

4. Wipe out the pan and add the remaining butter. Cook over moderate heat until beginning to brown, then add the lemon juice and herbs. When the lemon juice is added, the butter will bubble up and sizzle. Pour immediately over the fish and serve with lemon wedges.

Step 1 Trim the trout tails with scissors to make them neater.

Step 2 Coat trout in flour, shaking off excess.

Step 3 Brown the trout on both sides. Dorsal fin will pull out easily when done.

Cook's Notes

Time
Preparation takes 15-20 minutes, cooking takes 5-8 minutes per side for the fish and about 5 minutes to brown the butter.

Preparation
If trout is coated in flour too soon before cooking it will become soggy.

Serving Ideas
Serve with new potatoes and peeled, cubed cucumber quickly sautéed in butter and chopped dill.

SERVES 6

ROGNONS À LA DIJONNAISE

Veal kidneys are lighter in color and milder in flavor than lamb's kidneys. Since they must be quickly cooked, kidneys make an ideal sauté dish.

¼ cup unsalted butter
3-4 whole veal kidneys
1-2 shallots, finely chopped
1 cup dry white wine
⅓ cup butter, softened
3 tbsps Dijon mustard
Salt, pepper and lemon juice to taste
2 tbsps chopped parsley

1. Melt the unsalted butter in a large sauté pan. Cut the kidneys into 1 inch pieces and remove any fat or core. When the butter stops foaming, add the kidneys and sauté them, uncovered, until they are light brown on all sides, about 10 minutes. Remove the kidneys from the pan and keep them warm.

2. Add the shallots to the pan and cook for about 1 minute, stirring frequently. Add the wine and bring to the boil, stirring constantly and scraping the pan to remove any browned juices. Allow to boil rapidly for 3-4 minutes until the wine is reduced to about 3 tbsps. Remove the pan from the heat.

3. Mix the remaining butter with the mustard, add salt and pepper and whisk the mixture into the reduced sauce. Return the kidneys to the pan, add the lemon juice and parsley and cook over low heat for 1-2 minutes to heat through. Serve immediately.

Step 1 Slice the kidneys and remove any fat or core.

Step 2 Add wine to the pan and scrape to remove browned juices (deglaze).

Step 3 Whisk the butter and mustard mixture gradually into the reduced sauce.

Cook's Notes

Variations
If veal kidneys are not available, use lamb kidneys instead.

Time
Preparation takes about 25 minutes, cooking 15-17 minutes.

Cook's Tip
Use unsalted butter for sautéeing or shallow frying because it does not burn as quickly as salted butter.

Watchpoint
Kidneys and all offal need careful, quick cooking or they will toughen.

SERVES 6

CARBONNADE À LA FLAMANDE

This carbonnade is a rich stew cooked in the
Flemish style with dark beer.

2 tbsps oil
1½lbs chuck steak
1 large onion, thinly sliced
2 tbsps flour
1 clove garlic, crushed
1 cup brown ale
1 cup hot water
Bouquet garni, salt and pepper
Pinch sugar and nutmeg
Dash red wine vinegar
6 slices French bread cut about ½ inch thick
French or Dijon mustard

1. Preheat the oven to 325°F. Place the oil in a large, heavy-based frying pan. Cut the meat into 2 inch pieces and brown quickly on both sides in the oil. Brown the meat 5-6 pieces at a time to avoid crowding the pan.

2. Remove the meat when browned, lower the heat and add the onion. Cook until the onion is beginning to soften and color. Stir in the flour and add the garlic. Add the hot water and ale.

3. Add the bouquet garni, season with salt and pepper, add the sugar, nutmeg and vinegar. Bring to the boil on top of the stove. Transfer to an ovenproof casserole with the meat, cover and cook in the oven for 2-2½ hours.

4. Fifteen minutes before serving, skim off any fat from the surface and reserve it. Spread the mustard on the bread and spoon some of the fat over each slice.

Step 1 Cut the meat into 2 inch pieces and brown in the oil.

Step 4 Spread the bread with mustard and spoon reserved fat over each slice.

Step 5 Place bread on top of casserole and push down slightly.

5. Place the bread on top of the casserole, pushing it down slightly. Cook a further 15-20 minutes, uncovered, or until the bread is browned and crisp.

Cook's Notes

Time
Preparation takes about 30 minutes, cooking takes 2-2¾ hours.

Watchpoint
Add the ale gradually to the hot casserole as it may foam up and boil over.

Preparation
The casserole may be prepared in advance and the bread added just before reheating to serve.

Variations
Add carrots or mushrooms, if desired.

Freezing
Prepare the casserole in advance without the bread topping. Cool it completely, pour into a freezer container, cover, label and freeze for up to 3 months.

SERVES 4-6

FILET DE PORC AUX PRUNEAUX

Tours, situated on the River Loire, is where this dish originated. It is a rich dish with its creamy sauce and wine-soaked prunes.

2-3 small pork tenderloins
1lb pitted prunes
2 cups white wine
3 tbsps butter or margarine
1-2 tbsps flour
Salt and pepper
1 tbsp redcurrant jelly
1 cup heavy cream

1. Soak the prunes in the white wine for about 1 hour and then put them into a very low oven to soften further. If the prunes are the ready-softened variety, soak for 20 minutes and omit the oven cooking.

2. Slice the pork fillet on the diagonal into 1-inch-thick pieces. Flatten them slightly with the palm of the hand. Dredge them with the flour, and melt the butter in a heavy pan. When the butter is foaming, put in the pork and cook until lightly browned on both sides. It may be necessary to cook the pork fillet in several batches.

3. Add half the soaking liquid from the prunes, cover the pan and cook very gently on moderate heat for about 45 minutes. If necessary, add more wine from the prunes while the pork is cooking.

4. When the pork is tender, pour liquid into a small saucepan and bring to the boil. Reduce by about ¼ and add the redcurrant jelly. Stir until dissolved and then add the cream. Bring the sauce back to the boil and allow to boil rapidly, stirring frequently. When the sauce is reduced and

Step 1 Cook the prunes in wine until softened.

Step 2 Slice the pork fillet and flatten the slices with the palm of the hand.

Step 4 Whisk the redcurrant jelly into the boiling sauce.

thickened slightly, pour over the meat and reheat. Add the prunes and transfer to a serving dish. Sprinkle with chopped parsley if desired.

Cook's Notes

Variation
Substitute water or stock for half of the wine measurement.

Time
Preparation about 25 minutes, cooking about 45 minutes.

Watchpoint
Pork fillet is very lean meat and can easily dry out. Be careful not to over-cook and make sure to use enough liquid.

Cook's Tip
Pork fillet may be cooked in a moderate oven for the same length of time.

SERVES 6

RAGOÛT DE VEAU MARENGO

There is an Italian influence evident in this stew recipe.
Pie veal is relatively inexpensive, thus making this
recipe easier on the budget than most veal dishes.

3lbs lean pie veal
4 tbsps flour, mixed with salt and pepper
4 tbsps olive oil
2 shallots, finely chopped
½ clove garlic, crushed
⅓ cup dry white wine
1 cup brown stock
8oz canned tomatoes, drained and crushed
1 bouquet garni
2 strips lemon peel
4oz mushrooms, whole if small, quartered if large
3 tbsps butter or margarine
2 tbsps chopped parsley (optional)

Step 2 Brown the veal well on all sides.

Step 3 Cook the shallots and garlic gently until softened but not colored.

Step 4 Tilt the pan to make it easier to skim off excess fat.

1. Preheat oven to 325°F. Dredge the pieces of veal with the seasoned flour.

2. Pour the oil into a large sauté pan or heatproof casserole and place over a moderate heat. When the oil is hot, cook the veal 5-10 pieces at a time, depending upon the size of the pan. Brown the veal well on all sides, remove from the pan and set aside.

3. Add the shallots and garlic to the pan, lower the heat and cook until softened, but not colored. Return the veal to the pan, add the wine, stock, tomatoes, bouquet garni and lemon peel. Bring to the boil on top of the stove, cover and cook in the oven for 1¼ hours, or until the veal is tender.

4. Meanwhile, melt the remaining butter in a frying pan and add the mushrooms and toss over a moderate heat for 2-3 minutes, stirring occasionally. When the veal is cooked, skim the surface of the sauce to remove excess fat and add the mushrooms with their cooking liquid to the veal. Cook for a further 10-15 minutes then remove the bouquet garni and the lemon peel.

5. Transfer the veal and mushrooms to a serving dish and reduce the sauce to about 1½ cups by boiling rapidly. Adjust the seasoning and pour the sauce over the veal and mushrooms before serving. Reheat if necessary and garnish with chopped parsley, if desired.

Cook's Notes

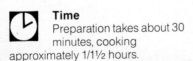

Time
Preparation takes about 30 minutes, cooking approximately 1/1½ hours.

Serving Ideas
Serve with plain boiled potatoes, pasta or rice.

Watchpoint
Do not allow garlic to brown as it will turn bitter.

SERVES 6

NAVARIN PRINTANIER

This is a ragôut or brown stew traditionally made with
mutton chops. Substitute lamb for a milder taste.
Printanier means that a selection of vegetables is added.

⅓ cup vegetable oil
12 even-sized lamb cutlets
Flour mixed with salt, pepper and a pinch dried thyme
2 shallots, finely chopped
1 clove garlic, crushed
2 cups brown stock
½ cup dry white wine
5 tomatoes, peeled, seeded and coarsely chopped
1 bouquet garni

Spring Vegetables

12 new potatoes, scrubbed but not peeled
8 baby carrots, scraped (if green tops are in good
    condition, leave on)
6 small turnips, peeled and left whole
12oz frozen petits pois
8oz green beans cut into 1 inch lengths on the diagonal
12 green onions, roots ends trimmed and green tops
    trimmed about 3 inches from the ends
1 tbsps chopped parsley (optional)

Remove the cores
from the
tomatoes.

Plunge into
boiling water for a
few seconds.

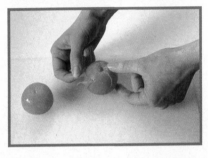

Refresh in cold
water then peel
off skins.

1. Preheat the oven to 350°F. Heat about half the oil in a large, heavy-based frying pan. Dredge the lamb cutlets with the flour mixture, shaking off the excess. Brown the lamb cutlets 4 at a time, adding more oil if necessary. When the cutlets are brown on all sides, remove them to a heavy casserole.

2. Remove most of the oil from the pan and cook the shallots and garlic over moderate heat, stirring constantly. Add the stock and bring to the boil, scraping the bottom of the pan to remove the browned meat juices. Allow to boil rapidly to reduce slightly, then add the tomatoes.

3. Pour the sauce over the lamb, turning the cutlets to coat all of them with the sauce. Add the bouquet garni, cover tightly and cook in the oven for about 30 minutes, or until the lamb is tender.

4. After about 10 minutes, add the potatoes and carrots to the lamb.

5. Add the turnips, green beans, peas and green onions 15 minutes before the end of cooking time.

6. After 30 minutes, remove the lamb and any vegetables that are tender. Boil the sauce rapidly to reduce it and cook any vegetables that need extra time. Pour the sauce over the lamb and vegetables to serve and sprinkle with chopped parsley, if desired.

Cook's Notes

Variations
Substitute other vegetables as desired, but always cook root vegetables first. Canned tomatoes may be substituted for fresh ones.

Time
Preparation takes 30-40 minutes, cooking about 30-35 minutes.

SERVES 6

Poires au Vin Rouge

A marvellous recipe for using firm cooking pears to their
best advantage. They look beautiful served in a glass bowl.

2 cups dry red wine
Juice of half lemon
1 strip lemon peel
1 cup sugar
1 small piece stick cinnamon
6 small ripe but firm pears, peeled, but with the
   stalks left on

1. Bring the wine, lemon juice and peel, sugar and cinnamon to the boil in a deep saucepan or ovenproof casserole that will accommodate 6 pears snugly. Stir until the sugar dissolves and then allow to boil rapidly for 1 minute.

2. Peel the pears lengthwise and remove the small eye from the bottom of each pear. Place the pears upright in the simmering wine. Allow to cook slowly for 20 minutes, or until they are soft but not mushy. If the syrup does not completely cover the pears, allow the pears to cook on their sides and turn and baste them frequently. Cool the pears in the syrup until lukewarm and then remove them. Remove the cinnamon stick and the lemon peel and discard.

3. If the syrup is still very thin, remove pears, boil to reduce slightly or mix 1 tbsp arrowroot with a little cold water, add some of the warm syrup and return the arrowroot to the rest of the syrup. Bring to the boil, stirring constantly until thickened and cleared. Spoon the syrup over the pears and refrigerate or serve warm. Pears may be decorated with slivered toasted almonds and served with lightly whipped cream if desired.

Step 2 Peel the pears lengthwise and remove the eye from the bottom.

Step 2 Place the pears in the simmering wine, upright or on their sides.

Step 3 Spoon the syrup over the pears and decorate with almonds.

Cook's Notes

Variations
Pears may be cooked au Vin Blanc with a dry white wine or in fruit juice.

Cook's Tip
Add a few drops of red food coloring to the syrup if the pears appear too pale when cooked.

Time
Preparation takes about 25 minutes, cooking 20 minutes.

SERVES 6

MOUSSE AU CHOCOLAT BASQUE

This mousse is a dark chocolate mixture which
sets to a rich cream in the refrigerator.

6oz semi-sweet chocolate
Scant ⅓ cup water
1 tbsp butter
3 eggs, separated
2 tbsps rum

1. Chop the chocolate into small pieces and combine with the water in a heavy-based saucepan. Cook over very gentle heat so that the chocolate and water form a thick cream. Remove from the heat, allow to cool slightly and then beat in the butter.

2. Add the rum and beat in the egg yolks one at a time.

Step 1 Melt chopped chocolate in water over gentle heat.

Step 2 Beat in egg yolks one at a time.

Step 3 Fold lightly whipped egg whites into the chocolate mixture.

3. Whip the egg whites until stiff but not dry and fold thoroughly into the chocolate mixture. Pour into small pots or custard cups and chill overnight. Finish with whipped cream and chocolate curls to serve, if desired.

Cook's Notes

Watchpoint
Never melt chocolate over direct heat without using some liquid. Do not over-whip egg whites; this will make the mousse grainy in texture.

Variations
Add strong coffee in place of water, or flavor with grated orange rind. Use juice instead of the water and add Grand Marnier instead of rum.

Time
Preparation takes 20 minutes, cooking takes approximately 10 minutes to melt the chocolate.

SERVES 6

SOUFFLÉ AU CITRON FROID

A cold soufflé is really a mousse in disguise. It doesn't
"rise" in the refrigerator, but is set above the rim of
its dish with the help of a paper collar and gelatine.

3 eggs, separated
¾ cup sugar
Grated rind and juice of 2 small lemons
1 tbsp gelatine dissolved in 3-4 tbsps water
¾ cup cream, lightly whipped

Decoration

½ cup cream, whipped
Thin strips lemon rind or lemon twists
Finely chopped almonds or pistachios

1. Tie a double thickness of wax paper around a soufflé
dish to stand about 3 inches above the rim of the dish.

2. Beat the egg yolks in a large bowl until thick and lemon
colored. Add the sugar gradually and then the lemon rind
and juice. Set the bowl over a pan of hot water and whisk
until the mixture is thick and leaves a ribbon·trail. Remove
the bowl from the heat and whisk a few minutes longer.

3. Melt the gelatine and the water until clear, pour into the
lemon mixture and stir thoroughly. Set the bowl over ice and
stir until beginning to thicken.

4. Whip the egg whites until stiff but not dry and fold into
the lemon mixture along with the lightly whipped cream.
Pour into the prepared soufflé dish and chill in the
refrigerator until the gelatine sets completely. To serve, peel
off the paper carefully and spread some of the cream on the
sides of the mixture. Press finely chopped nuts into the
cream. Pipe the remaining cream into rosettes on top of the
soufflé and decorate with strips of rind or lemon twists.

Step 2 When
thick enough,
mixture will leave
a ribbon trail.

Step 4 Fold the
egg whites and
cream into the
mixture and pour
into the prepared
dish.

Step 4 Peel off
the paper
carefully.

Cook's Notes

Time
Preparation takes about 25-30
minutes.

Watchpoint
Do not allow gelatine to boil; it
will lose its setting qualities.

Cook's Tip
If gelatine sets before cream
and egg whites are added,
gently reheat the lemon mixture,
stirring constantly until soft again.

Preparation
Do not fill the dish more than
1½ inches above the rim of
the dish or, once decorated, the
mixture will collapse.

SERVES 6

CRÊPES AU
CHOCOLAT ET FRAMBOISES

Crêpes Suzette may be more famous, but these.
filled with chocolate and raspberry, are incredibly delicious.

Crêpe Batter

1½ cups milk and water mixed
4 eggs
Pinch salt
2 cups all-purpose flour, sifted
1 tbsp sugar
4 tbsps melted butter or oil

Filling

8oz semi-sweet dessert chocolate, grated
4oz seedless raspberry jam
Whipped cream and chopped, browned hazelnuts

1. Put all the ingredients for the crêpes into a food processor or blender and process for about 1 minute, pushing down the sides occasionally. Process a few seconds more to blend thoroughly. Leave, covered, in a cool place for 30 minutes to 1 hour. The consistency of the batter should be that of thin cream. Add more milk if necessary. Brush a crêpe pan or small frying pan lightly with oil and place over high heat. When a slight haze forms, pour a large spoonful of the batter into the pan and swirl the pan to cover the base. Pour out any excess into a separate bowl. Cook on one side until just beginning to brown around the edges. Turn over and cook on the other side until lightly speckled with brown. Slide each crêpe onto a plate and repeat using the remaining batter. Reheat the pan occasionally in between cooking each crêpe. The amount of batter should make 12 crêpes.

Step 1 Cook until edges are brown then turn over.

Step 1 When underside is lightly speckled with brown, slide onto a plate.

2. As the crêpes are cooked, sprinkle them evenly with grated chocolate and divide the raspberry jam among all the crêpes. Roll them up so that the jam shows at the ends, or fold into triangles.

3. Reheat in a moderate oven for about 10 minutes before serving. Top with whipped cream and a sprinkling of browned nuts.

Cook's Notes

Time
Preparation takes about 30 minutes, cooking takes about 30 minutes.

Variation
To make savory crêpes, leave out the sugar but prepare them in the same way.

Watchpoint
Batter works best when only one quarter water to three quarters milk used in the mixture. The batter must stand for at least 30 minutes before use to allow it too thicken properly.

Freezing
Allow crêpes to cool completely and stack between sheets of nonstick or wax paper. Place in a plastic bag and freeze for up to 3 months. Defrost completely but separate and reheat as needed.

MAKES 12

ECLAIRS

Think of French pastry and eclairs immediately spring
to mind. French patisseries - pastry shops - sell
them filled and iced in many different flavors.

Choux Pastry

⅞ cup water
⅓ cup butter or margarine
¾ cup all-purpose flour, sifted
3 eggs

Crème Patissière

1 whole egg
1 egg yolk
¼ cup sugar
1 tbsp cornstarch
1½ tbsps flour
1 cup milk
Few drops vanilla extract

Glacé Icing

1lb confectioners' sugar
Hot water
Few drops vanilla extract

1. Preheat the oven to 350°F.

2. Combine the water and butter for the pastry in a deep saucepan and bring to the boil. Once boiling rapidly, take the pan off the heat. Stir in the flour all at once and beat just until the mixture leaves the sides of the pan. Spread out onto a plate to cool. When cool, return to the saucepan and gradually add the beaten egg. Beat in well in between each addition of egg until the paste is smooth and shiny – should be of soft dropping consistency, but holding its shape well. It may not be necessary to add all the egg. Pipe or spoon into strips of about 3 inches long, spaced well apart on lightly-greased baking sheets.

3. Sprinkle the sheets lightly with water and place in the oven. Immediately increase oven temperature to 375°F.

Step 6 Cut the eclairs almost in half. Pipe or spoon in the crème patissière.

Make sure the pastry is very crisp before removing it from the oven, this will take about 20-30 minutes cooking time. If the pastry is not crisp, return to the oven for a further 5 minutes.

4. To prepare the Crème Patissière, separate the whole egg and reserve the white. Mix the egg yolks and sugar together, sift in the flours and add about half the milk, stirring well. Bring the remainder of the milk to the boil and pour onto the yolk mixture, stirring constantly. Return the mixture to the pan and stir over heat until boiling point is reached. Take off the heat and whip the egg white until stiff but not dry. Fold the egg white into the mixture and return to the heat. Cook gently for about 1 minute, stirring occasionally. Add the vanilla extract at this point. Pour the mixture into a bowl and press a sheet of wax paper directly onto the surface of the crème and leave it to cool.

5. Sift the confectioners' sugar into a bowl and add hot water, stirring constantly until the mixture is of thick coating consistency. The icing should cover the back of a wooden spoon but run off slowly. Add the vanilla extract.

6. To assemble the eclairs, cut the choux pastry almost in half lengthwise and either pipe or spoon in the Crème Patissière. Using a large spoon, coat the top of each eclair with a smooth layer of glacé icing. Allow the icing to set before serving.

Cook's Notes

Time
Preparation takes about 40 minutes, cooking takes about 30-40 minutes.

Cook's Tip
Water sprinkled on the baking sheet creates steam to help pastry rise.

Preparation
1-2 tsps oil added to the icing will keep it shiny when set.

INDEX

ACKNOWLEDGMENT
The publishers wish to thank the following suppliers
for their kind assistance:
Corning Ltd for providing Pyrex and other cookware.
Habasco International Ltd for the loan of basketware.
Stent (Pottery) Ltd for the loan of glazed pottery oven-
to-table ware.

Compiled by Judith Ferguson
Photographed by Peter Barry
Designed by Philip Clucas and Sara Cooper
Recipes Prepared for Photography by
Jacqueline Bellefontaine